WHAT I'VE LEARNED ABOUT
YOUR JOB SEARCH
THAT YOU MAY NOT KNOW

Jeff Morris
Founder of
CareerDFW.org and CareerUSA.org
Giving you the tools you need to land your next great opportunity.™

WHAT I'VE LEARNED ABOUT
YOUR JOB SEARCH
THAT YOU MAY NOT KNOW

© 2012 by Jeff Morris

Visit the website at www.CareerDFW.org or www.CareerUSA.org

Printed in the United States of America

ISBN-13: 978-1479213429
ISBN-10: 147921342X

First Printing: 2012
r1.4

Contents

Preface

Jeff Morris is an operations and organizations professional with more than 20 years in a light manufacturing, quick-turn environment. He has extensive customer service and team building experience. Jeff is skilled in identifying and implementing solutions (lean manufacturing), facilitating staff development and increasing productivity by incorporating Six Sigma.

Jeff moved to Texas in 1987 and worked for one company for more than 13 years before being laid off. Since then, he has been hired, laid off, hired, laid off, hired (Jeff quit this job after 90 days, since they did not pay their bills and it is hard to work with no power), hired again and laid off.

In 2007, Jeff started facilitating the North Dallas / Plano Career Focus Group. The group had been meeting since 2001 and Jeff took over for the previous facilitator, who landed a job. The group assisted in placing more than 210 people in new jobs in 2010, and more than 160 in 2011.

In 2008, Jeff Morris founded CareerDFW.org, a website created to assist the unemployed and underemployed in the DFW area. CareerDFW became a 501(c)(3) public charity nonprofit in 2009. CareerDFW is 100 percent run by volunteers, and currently has no full or part-time employees. Jeff has spoken to more than 50 groups in the DFW area in the past three years about CareerDFW.

In 2012, Jeff launched CareerUSA.org, a website like CareerDFW.org, to help those in other communities across the United States.

Jeff is dual degreed in broadcasting and meteorology from Western Kentucky University. He currently lives in Dallas with his wife, Melanie, and their two children.

Acknowledgments

Many thanks to my wife, Melanie, for her support with CareerDFW.org and CareerUSA.org, editing and adding her comments and opinions to this book and the websites. Thanks also to my children, Alexandra and Mitchell, for their help and support with CareerDFW.org and CareerUSA.org.

Thanks to Beth Kohler for proofreading and editing the first draft of this book. Thanks also to Michelle Kreitman for the final corrections. I never realized the amount of attention to detail that a great proofreader provides.

Thanks to Dan White of Art Avenue Graphics in Oklahoma City, OK, for the cover layout. www.ArtAvenueGraphics.com

Thanks to those who have spoken at the North Dallas/Plano Career Focus Group over the past few years: Locke Alderson, Dean Allred, Rodney Anderson, Mark Arnold, Paula Asinof, Rich Ballner, Richard Best, Michelle Botzau, Beth Boyer, Mina Brown, Mitch Byers, Doug Caldwell, Mike Chapman, John Childers, Roxanne Clary, Mike Coffey, Jeff Crilley, Stephanie Cross, Lori Darley, Tom Davis, David Dennard, Nancy Driver, Dr. Glen Earl, David Ellis, Richard Fine, Peter Gailey, Ruth Glover, Marie Guthrie, Kathy Gutierrez, Elaine Hamm, Gail Herson, Susan Holley, Linda Howard, Mike Ingram, Tom Jackson, Carolann Jacobs, John Jacobs, Danielle Kunkle, David Lanners, Tonja LaFrenz, Frank Lee, Bob Maher, Shannon Markle, Jose Martinez-Garriga, Terri Maxwell, Ellen Miller, Penny Miller, Sue Mintz, Bob Mosley, Jan Moorman, John Moorman, Paula Neff, Brad Nelson, Michael Newman, Dennis O'Hagan, Sylvia Pas, John Paul, John Prey, James Prince, Walt Purkey, Miguel Richards, Glen Ruby, Todd Sayles, Fred Shlesinger, Stu Slippen, Bob Snelling, Dirk Spencer, Gary Spinell, David Swinney, Rob Taylor, James Tucker, Paul Turner, Pam Venne, Tim Wackel, Bill Wallace, Russ Yaquinto, Marcia Zidle, Steve Zipkoff and anyone else I may have overlooked. **I have learned something from each of you.**

Thanks to these other great people and career groups who have and continue to help the unemployed and have offered me advice and help over the years:

Bill Brewer, Gail Bridgeman, CareerConnection, Jim Curry, Rick Gillis, Sue Heusing, Gail Houston, Jewish Family Services Employment Group, Tom Leverenz, Lisa Miller, Claire Mullins, Lynn Pittman, Rex Saoit, Mark Siegel, Foster Williams, and all the great volunteer leaders who take time out of their schedule to assist and lead the career groups in the DFW area.

Thanks to the Board of Directors of CareerDFW: Dr. Glen Earl, Dennis O'Hagan and Richard Solomon.

Thanks to those of you who have visited the website and sent compliments about it.

Finally, the biggest thanks goes to those of you who have donated to CareerDFW. Your support in helping CareerDFW to assist those in our area is greatly appreciated.

Introduction

Over the past several years, I have watched many people get laid off and show up at a career group with a blank look on their face ... *what do I do next?* These people are lost. They have not had to look for a job in 15, 20 or 25 years. They do not have a resume. They do not even have a personal email account, having relied on their company's email system. They are stumped.

I have also seen many people land their next great opportunity. How did they do it? That is what I want to explore in this book. Some of the topics will be short. Other will go into more detail. You may already know some of these career tips, and hopefully you will learn some new ones.

Where are jobs found?

I have heard these numbers over and over again from speakers in the past several years:
5 to10 percent of jobs are found on the Internet
10 to15 percent of jobs are found using a recruiter
75 to 80 percent of jobs are found through networking

You should spend your job search time where you get the biggest result.

If you had $100 and went to the bank to invest in a CD, would you get the CD that offered a 5 percent, 10 percent or 75 percent return? Surely you would get the CD with the largest return.

Networking offers you the biggest return so spend the most time on it. Find networking groups in your area. Check with the local Chamber of Commerce. They meet monthly or more often. Find the professional groups in your area of expertise. No matter what your field, there is probably a professional group for it. For example, in the DFW area, there is a monthly meeting of professional wedding planners.

Networking includes formal opportunities such as informational interviews, Toastmasters, job fairs and Jaycees. It also includes informal opportunities such as volunteering, going to the grocery store, attending parties, talking to other parents on the soccer sidelines, etc.

Anything that gets you out of the house and talking to others is networking.

I have divided this book into five sections...
> Section 1: Calendar–What Do I Do First?
> Section 2: Your Digital Footprint
> Section 3: Networking
> Section 4: Interviewing
> Section 5: Other Career Tips

One of the hundreds of speakers I've heard over the past several years started his talk with: *"You only have to take one tip away from here, and do it, for my presentation to be a success."*

I really do not remember what his subject was. What I took away from his presentation was—did you guess it? - be sure to take at least one thing away from every speaker I hear and implement it. After every speaker's presentation, I stop and think about what they said. What was the point of their talk? What is the one thing I will take away from today and implement in my life?

This book is a collection of those points. In the Acknowledgments I have listed many of the speakers I have heard over the years. I know I have left out many, many more, but it would be nice to include everyone I have ever listened to since I first started working. Each one of those speakers have shared wonderful information.

I hope that you will find a least one tip from this book that really hits you and "DO IT!"

Good luck and go land that next great opportunity!

Section One

Calendar—What Do I Do First?

The first week:
1) File for unemployment (if you have been working).
2) Make sure you have a professional job search email address.
3) Make yourself a nametag.
4) Work on your resume.
5) Make sure your LinkedIn profile is up to date.
6) Get your business cards.
7) Decompress.

The first 30 days:
1) Look at your health insurance plan, COBRA, or other options.
2) Send an email to your network.
3) Start a workout routine.
4) Develop a daily/weekly schedule and stick with it.
5) Develop 10- and 30-second introductions.
6) Find the networking groups that fit your needs.
7) Post your resume to the "main" job boards.
8) Start a job log to keep track of your opportunities.

The first 60 to 90 days:
1) Hone your 30-second introduction and review monthly.
2) Keep your LinkedIn profile active.
   a. Add connections.
   b. Add and update the Reading List application.
   c. Fine-tune expertise descriptions.
   d. Load examples of your work.
   e. Research who you want to be and clone their profile.
3) Seek out professional groups and join them. (They all need volunteers.) They can be industry specific or not (e.g. Toastmasters, Rotary, etc.) Do not just

focus on career networking groups—only the unemployed are usually there.

4) Evaluate your image—haircut, glasses, clothing, diet, general appearance.
5) Join or create an accountability group.
6) Reset priorities—what are you doing right and wrong?—alter course if needed.
7) **Keep a reading list.
8) **Pursue a hobby.
9) **Nurture your spirit (read, exercise, pray, pursue a hobby, etc.)
10) **Volunteer.

** These things keep you interesting and give you connections and things to talk about.

Section Two

Your Digital Footprint

What is your digital footprint?

Your digital footprint is anything that someone could find out about you on the Internet. When someone searches your name on Google or Bing or another search engine, what comes up?

Do YOU know? You'd better!

You want to expand your digital footprint to increase your chances of being found. In this way you can take some control of the internet by controlling your profile and the information that others can find out about you.

Shift your paradigm to "being found," not just finding others or other opportunities.

This is the new model and you must use the Internet as your tool to facilitate this.

Other ways to expand your digital footprint:

1) LinkedIn—if you are not on it, get on it.
2) Have a personal website.
3) Create a Twitter account—Twitter is a matter of being followed and following others.
4) Create a blog—LinkedIn does this for you easily via WordPress, which provides templates and easy ways to push your content to Facebook, Twitter, RSS feeds and more. This is a great way to let others know what you know.
5) Write book reviews on Amazon.
6) Create a Google profile—Google yourself to see where you pop up. A sure way to get yourself on page one is to create a Google profile. Keep it updated! Make sure that all of your other URL's

(web addresses) from this list are listed on your Google profile.

7) Facebook—think of this as your digital billboard.

Make sure that you use the same picture, the same email, the same name (i.e. Joe or Joseph) across all the platforms.

Remember that you are creating a brand for yourself.

People naturally want to network with, recruit, hire and contact the people who have the greatest professional presence on the web.

Where should you post your resume?

Remember that the more places on the Internet you post your resume, the more places you need to change your resume (if you remember where you posted it).

I believe that you should limit the number of places you post your resume and consider the following list:

1) Monster
2) CareerBuilder
3) LinkedIn
4) Ladders—for higher level professionals (six-figure salary)
5) Dice—for technical professionals
6) Your personal website (if you have one)

Why only these? Only 5-10 percent of jobs are found on the internet.

Don't spend a lot of time worrying about updating something that gives you a small return.

Of course you should always customize your resume for the job you are applying for, and always use the same keywords, job title, etc. as the job posting. No two resumes should be the same unless you are applying for the same job.

Refresh your posted resume.

Many people post resumes on Monster, CareerBuilder or some other website and never update them. Here's what happens—your resume goes to the bottom of the pile. Everyone with a newer date/time stamped resume will be above you. When you look at your resume online, you will be able to see the last date it was edited or updated.

What do you update? All you have to do is edit your posted resume. Add a space ... take away a space. Add a date ... change a date. Add a period ... take away a period. Do something and save it. When you do, you are now at the top of the pile again.

You should update your resume at least twice a week. I recommend **Sunday** and **Wednesday** nights.

I know a person who updated his online resume every weekday morning between 6 and 7 am. The result was that he received many phone calls. Why? Because when the recruiter arrived at the office at 8 a.m. and ran a query for a skill set, guess whose resume was at the top?

Convert your cover letter and resume to a PDF when you send it.

My resume document is three pages. The first page is a cover letter and the second and third pages are my two-page resume all together in one document.

Now, when you send a hiring manager your resume and a cover letter, I recommend converting it to a PDF file. There are a couple of reasons for this.

First, your cover letter and resume will be together no matter where the document floats around in a company. The document is one file. The company cannot break it up. (Well, they could with the right software.) No matter who sees your resume, they will see your cover letter also.

Second, the formatting will stay just as you want it to be. When you send a Word document to others, unless they have the same printer as yours, their default printer will cause the Word document to format for their printer. This may (and usually does) change the margins, tabs, spacing, font, email format, etc.

I asked a career focus group to send me their resume for a presentation I was going to give to the group. More than 60 percent of the resumes people sent me looked unprofessional, due to spacing, tab and margin problems. I know each person sent me what they intended for me to see from their computer, but when I opened it on my computer, it did not look right. The resumes of the two people who sent me a PDF file looked just as they intended it to.

Third, when you send your cover letter and resume to a company as one PDF document, you save it in your files and you can easily refer to it when they give you a call. And since I customize my resume for each job description, I know what I have sent for each job.

Now, it is true that you cannot upload a PDF file to many of the applicant tracking systems. You need your Word document to do that. But when you have someone's email address, you should send a PDF file so your resume will always look just like YOU want it to look.

Create a dedicated email account.

You should have a dedicated email account for your job search that is separate from your personal account. I recommend a Yahoo or Gmail account. Some people will say having an AOL account shows your age. AOL was great in the 90's, but not now.

You do not want to use a swbell.com, sbcglobal.net, att.net, rr.com, verizon.net, etc., address. Why? What if you move? The company that provides your current service may not offer service where you move, so your email address will be gone.

Back in the days of dial-up, I had an email account for several years with iAmerica, until the company sent me an overnight letter telling me that the company had been sold (to another Internet company) and my email address would be turned off in 30 days. There was no offer to switch to the other company, "Goodbye, so long, farewell!" I opened two Yahoo accounts and have used them since. The nice thing is that I can check my email account anywhere there is a computer, anywhere in the world. Yes, I also have an email address through my DSL provider, but I never use it.

Google was not available when I opened my Yahoo accounts. The nice thing about a Gmail account is that you have free POP forwarding. If you know what POP forwarding is, you may want to open a Gmail account; otherwise, it doesn't matter whether you choose Yahoo or Gmail. (If you want to learn more about POP forwarding, conduct a search on Google or Wikipedia.) There are other providers, including Hotmail and others. You will need to check them out and ask others for their opinion (a good way to start a conversation and network!).

Make sure your email address looks professional. You do not want to be partyhard@ or hotmama@. (Those can be your personal email account but not for the job search.)

Do not use smithfamily@ or johnmary@. How does the hiring person know that you are going to read the email if it looks like a family email address? **Never** share an email address for your job search. It should be private and unique to you. Personally, I never reply to a family email account. I just press Delete. How do I know who will read the message?

Select your first and last name or some combination of it like john.smith@ or johnsmith88@.

Make it look professional.

Once you get a job, keep checking your job search email account.

All the contacts you have made during your job search know you by this email address.

I know a person who landed a job. I saw a great lead for him and sent it to his email address. I did not hear back from him. Several months later, he sent me an email about a job opening from a different account. I replied back, asking if he got the lead I sent him a few months back. He replied, *"Now that I'm working, I stopped checking that account."*

I could not believe what I had just heard. Think of the job leads and contacts who could NO longer reach him. A year and a half later, after he was laid off again, I saw him at a career group and told him my feelings on the subject. It made sense to him now that he was laid off again.

This also applies if you are part of a Yahoo or Google Group. Instead of unsubscribing from the group, change your profile to web only or special notices only. This will stop the daily or individual emails, but you will still be part of the group.

What if you are not happy at your job and you are ready to start your job search again? Many career groups will want you to attend a meeting of the group before you can get invited back into the Yahoo group.

If you never unsubscribe, you can search for job leads and other career advice at any time.

Always check your spam or junk mail folder.

How often do you check your spam folder? Checking that folder should be the first thing you do every time you open your email account.

Why? If you check it each time you open your email account, you can quickly check the few messages that are in the folder and then delete them. If you wait and check the spam folder once a week, you could have hundreds of spam emails and just delete the entire group without noticing the email from a possible employer.

The first time you get an email from a new person, it may go directly into your spam folder. And by not checking that folder, you could be missing out on some great opportunities.

I know a person who only checked his spam folder once or twice a month. He found an offer letter for a job in his email spam folder. It had been sitting there for more than two weeks. He immediately called the company, but was told, "We are sorry. We did not hear back from you and offered the job to another candidate." How did this situation happen? The email came from the HR department, that had never sent him an email before and it went to his spam folder.

It only takes a minute and you will not be overwhelmed if you check your spam or junk mail folder every day (or a couple of times a day).

Your email should have a signature line with ALL of your details.

I get a lot of emails each day and I bet you do too. Sometimes, I have no idea who the email is from. The email says, "Please call me, Joe." I ask myself, *Joe who?* There is no signature line, no phone number, and I cannot tell by the email address who sent it. Do you think I call them back? You're right if you said no.

I am sure you have seen a signature line. It is the contact info at the end of an email, right under the name. At the minimum, it should have: Name (first and last), what you do (your profession), phone number, and your email address. You can also list your LinkedIn, website, blog and Twitter accounts.

It could look like this:

John Smith
Project Manager
Cell: 123-555-7890
Home: 555-555-7890
JohnSmith@myemail.com
LinkedIn: www.linkedin.com/in/johnsmith
Twitter: JohnSmith
Website: www.JohnSmith.info

Why put your email address in the contact info? You want to make it easy for the recipient to copy the info and put it into their address book.

Not sure how to add or edit your signature? Type signature in the help box of your email program and it will walk you through the process.

Are you using Gmail? Here is a hint. For some unknown reason (although Google may have one), Gmail will add your signature line at the very end of the entire message you send ... the very, very bottom. For example, I send you an email, and you reply. Your signature appears after my initial email, not after your reply (like most other email programs).

You can fix this and have your signature appear between your message and the email that was sent to you by doing the following:
1) Open Gmail.
2) Click on the setup wheel in the upper right.
3) Click on Labs.
4) Scroll down until you see Signature Tweaks.
5) Click the Enable button.
6) Scroll to the top or to the very bottom and click on Save.

Your signature will now appear after your text and not at the very bottom.

Remember, a signature line makes it easy to be contacted and looks professional.

LinkedIn—social networking on the Internet.

There are several ways to network on the Internet. LinkedIn can be a powerful tool both in your job search, and when you are employed. LinkedIn is your PROFESSIONAL profile. This is where you post your complete work profile. This is where you can keep in touch with those you may have worked with in the past. LinkedIn is now your Rolodex— available to you online wherever you are.

In the '80s, it was who you knew for your next opportunity.

In the '90s, it was who you knew and who they knew to find your next opportunity.

In the 21st century, it is who you know that they know, that they know and <u>do they know how much you know</u>. You may have heard of the game "Six Degrees of Separation from Kevin Bacon." With LinkedIn, it is three degrees of separation.

Who you know are your first degree connections, **who those 1st degree connections know** are your 2nd degree connections and **who those 2nd degree connections people know** are your 3rd degree connections.

Let's say you know 100 people, and they all know 100 people. This gives you 10,000 2nd degree connections. If they all know 100 people, you have 1 million 3rd degree connections. So your total connections are 1,010,100 people. That can be very powerful when conducting a job search. (This assumes that none of the connections know each other).

Make it easy to be contacted on LinkedIn.

As I will say over and over ... **make it easy to be found!**

When I first got on LinkedIn many years ago there was not a place to put your email address, birthday, phone number and other personal information. I wanted to make it easy to be found. So I put my contact info in my summary statement, which is one of the top modules. You can read a summary about me and you have my contact information before you read about my background.

Be sure to include your email address and phone number in your personal information module. You want people to find you and make it easy to contact you. How many profiles have you looked at that don't tell you how to contact the person?

What you need to know about LinkedIn.

Get your profile to 100 percent. To do this, you have to have a fairly complete profile. In February 2012, LinkedIn changed what you needed to get to 100 percent. Here is what you need now:

1. Add a profile photo.
2. List all the jobs or positions you've held, along with descriptions of your roles.
3. Include five or more skills on your profile.
4. Write a summary about yourself.
5. Fill out your industry and postal code.
6. Add where you went to school.
7. Have 50 or more connections: it's easier than you think to get connected!

Yes, you need to include your picture. Your picture—not Brad Pitt's or Angelina Jolie's, not your pet's and not one from your childhood. Also, please use just your picture and not you and your significant other. There are many names that are gender neutral and you do not want to confuse people. Besides, it does not look professional.

LinkedIn will allow you to upload a photo and then edit the picture by zooming in to just your face. It can be a family photo, or any other photo. Be sure to zoom in to your face. We want to see you. Make sure you cannot see someone else cut off in the picture. Zoom in so the picture is just your face and nothing else. When viewing the picture online, at the most it will be 1 inch by 1 inch.

If you do not have a lot of hair or it is really gray, just zoom in closer!

Some people will say not to load a photo because someone will discriminate against you. Look … everyone discriminates.

When you found your boyfriend, girlfriend, husband or wife, you picked him or her because they looked _____. Fill in the blank.

The same goes for the first 15 seconds of an in-person interview. If someone wants to reject you for how you look, you just saved yourself grief down the line.

Do NOT use the generic invitation that LinkedIn defaults to.

I have never figured out why LinkedIn puts anything in the invitation. They should force you to write something. You always want to write a personal note to the person you are trying to connect to, even something as simple as, *"I met you at the networking meeting last Friday. I would like to connect with you."*

You will see the abbreviation LION on some people's LinkedIn profile. LION stands for **L**inked**I**n **O**pen **N**etworker, which means that they will connect with anyone. They are just looking for numbers. Personally, I will only connect with people I have met or who write me a personal note explaining why we should connect.

Be sure to set your profile so ANYONE can find you.

You want to be found.

Go to the top right corner where you see your name and click on it. Then click on Settings. It may take you to the log in screen and ask you to enter your password. Your Settings page will appear. Click on the Profile tab on the lower left side and then select Privacy Controls. If you're looking for a job, let everyone see everything on your profile.

MAKE IT EASY TO BE FOUND!

Be sure to enter ALL of your email addresses into LinkedIn.

You never know who will be looking for you and they may know only one of your email addresses. When you ARE working, be sure to add the company email address to your list. Let's say you are dealing with a contact at work who only knows your work email address. When they try to contact you in LinkedIn, they may be asked to provide an email address. Not having all of those email addresses loaded in LinkedIn may keep them from being able to contact you.

Go to your Account tab (select your name at the top right and click settings) and select, Add & change email addresses.

You can have as many email addresses listed as you have accounts. Be sure to include them all and make sure you do this when you have access to the account. You cannot list email addresses for previous employers (since you will not be able to confirm the address).

You do get to select the primary account where you will receive emails. You can change this at any time.

How much information should I put on LinkedIn?

Put it ALL down. This is your five, seven, 10-page resume. You want to include everything you have done since your professional career started. We do not need to know about the paper route you had when you were in high school or the part-time job you had in college ... unless it relates to your career.

By doing this you are building opportunities for old co-workers to find you. They may be good or great contacts for your job search.

LinkedIn allows you to search for others who worked at the same company. That is a great way to add contacts.

LinkedIn Recommendations.

Before February 2012, you needed three recommendations to get your LinkedIn profile to 100 percent. This no longer applies, but it still can be helpful to have recommendations. Note that you can only get reviews from other people who are in LinkedIn.

First, when you get a recommendation, LinkedIn will ask you if you want to give a recommendation to the person who just gave you one. NO! Do not give one to and get one back from the same person. When I read a recommendation, I tend to click on the person who wrote it and see who has recommended that person. When I read them and see a recommendation from you for that person, something smells fishy. You have just patted each other on the back. This does not look good. If you feel the need to do this, have person 1 write an recommendation for person 2 and person 2 write one for person 3 and then have person 3 write one for person 1.

Second, most people have received reviews or evaluation forms from a former boss. Connect with that person on LinkedIn and ask them to write you a recommendation. Or even better … if you have a copy of the review, take statements from it, write a recommendation, send it to the other person and let them know that this is what they wrote in old reviews and ask if they would copy and paste it into a recommendation.

Third, would you put a bad recommendation on your profile? I bet not. Anyone looking at your profile will know this.

Remember, you get to approve or decline each and every recommendation. Make sure that the spelling is correct (I copy and paste the recommendation into Word and use the spell checker). Make sure you approve what the other person has said about you. You cannot edit or change what another person says in a recommendation for you. If needed, you can always contact the writer and ask them to revise the recommendation for a misspelling or incorrect fact.

Additionally, be cognizant of the nature of your relationship with the person who writes your recommendation. Having recommendations only from peers is not as powerful as a recommendation from a former boss. If you are in sales, the most powerful recommendations you can have are from the outside—your customers. These are harder to ask for and to receive than from anyone internally, e.g. your boss. But they are proportionately more impressive.

I have done a couple of different things in my career. Should I create a second LinkedIn account?

NO!!! You only want ONE account. As I said earlier, your profile should have ALL of your professional experiences on it. You can always edit your account if you want to change something.

I was helping someone who had two profiles, which also meant he had two different sets of connections. So when he was looking for a job, he had to check both accounts for contacts every time. When he finally decided that he wanted to close one account and only use the one with the most contacts, he accidentally deleted the wrong account and lost the account he wanted to keep. I could almost hear him crying on the other end of the phone.

LinkedIn is great for networking.

When you find a job on a job board, follow all the instructions in the posting. Then search LinkedIn to see who you (or your connections) may know at the company.

I saw a job ad in the newspaper a year ago. I followed the instructions, filled out the online application and emailed my resume to the address listed. Next, I went to LinkedIn and searched my contacts to see if they knew anyone at the company (corporate headquarters were in North Carolina). I had a 1st-degree connection that was connected to someone in sales at the company. I contacted my 1st degree connection and asked how well he knew the person in North Carolina. He knew him well and said he would contact his connection and have him contact me. That evening I received an email from that person and he offered to help. I sent him my resume that night. The next morning about 9:15 I received an email from my 2nd-degree contact telling me he just dropped off my resume to the Director of HR. At 9:45 a.m. I was talking to the Director of HR. In less than 24 hours, using LinkedIn, I had a phone interview.

You want to have your resume appear from as many places as possible on the HR manager's or hiring manager's desk.

Most people on LinkedIn will help you. (Those who don't help you most likely have never had to look for a job ... but they will one day!) You want to find out about the culture of the company, how they treat people and gain insight into what problems you may face if you're hired. How do you approach someone? Read the topic on informational interviewing. You will find it later in this book.

LinkedIn—check to see who has the position to see where the job fillers came from.

When using LinkedIn, here is one more thing you can do to get some background about the position that may be helpful. When you apply for a job at a company, search LinkedIn and see if that company/position comes up in LinkedIn. You will have an opportunity to see who has done the job in the past and what their background was. You may see things on their profile that may help in your quest for the position.

Section Three

Networking

Self-awareness—read this FIRST before you begin to network.

Reprinted with permission from Alison Wilkinson, 2012, Retrieved from URL:
http://www.360dtl.com/body-language-how-important-are-these-numbers-5538-7/

Body language. How important are these numbers 55, 38, 7?

We have all probably heard of the power of the above numbers in the way we communicate.

Let's remind you:

55% body language, 38% tone of voice, 7% actual words used.

Therefore we can deduce from this that when we communicate with people the impact we make comes down to:

How you look, How you sound, What you say

In fact 93% of our message is conveyed by the language of the body including the voice.

The "silent" language is very powerful and this can include things like:

Dress
Posture
Facial expressions
Eye contact
Hand, arm and leg movement
Touch
Spatial awareness
Bodily tension

In summary, this means that in those vital first 2 minutes that we have to make a first impression, this is determined mainly by how we present ourselves and how we say things rather than what we say.

If the "silent" language does not match the words we hear, we tend to believe the delivery rather than the words. This can mean that if the 55% "silent" language is not good then your audience will not stick around to hear anymore.

Most research suggests that words are used to communicate information whereas body language conveys our attitudes, feelings and emotions. People will make decisions as to whether or not to trust you, do business with you, whether they like you or not in the first 3 minutes of meeting you.

So make sure people are reading you correctly. Be conscious of your body language and become more aware of both your own body language but those of others.

Ask yourself the following: "What signals are people sending out and what signals am I sending out?"

With this in mind we need to think about open and closed body language.

Open body language is welcoming, relaxed and attentive. Your hands are usually in view, with open hands and good eye contact.

Closed body language is the opposite, with the gestures and movements closing the body in on itself. For example, crossing of the arms, little eye contact and tension in shoulders.

So in summary it is important that you remember the importance of the "silent" language you are projecting with your body language. Are you open or closed? What is the tone of your voice like?

Always remember **93**% of your message is conveyed through your body language and tone of voice.

Only **7**% is the words you actually say.

Network...Network...Network

There are different types of networking
    Going to unemployment networking groups
    Going to professional networking groups
    Meeting people at your place of worship
    Meeting people at your child's sporting event
    Talking to your friends and family
    Meeting people at a holiday event
    Meeting people at a school event
    Meeting people while shopping
    Meeting people on a plane
    Meeting people while standing in line

You have to get out and network! If you're sitting at home, you're not networking—networking must have other people involved.

As I have said before, 75 to 80 percent of jobs are found through networking.

"If you are not networking, you are not working (at job search)."

Let's take a look at some of the different types of networking:

Unemployment networking groups: These may be groups run by your local workforce unemployment office or sponsored by a religious or other organization. Most, if not all, of the people who come are unemployed. When you're at these types of meetings it is important to have target companies to mention; you never know whose spouse, parent, friend, etc. may work at a place where you want to get a foot in the door.

Professional networking groups: These are groups in your local area that are affiliated with a national organization.

35

They may offer continuing education credit or topical speakers. These groups are usually broken down by profession. Many of the members will be employed, making these types of meetings a great place to network. **It is not the most qualified person who gets the job, but the person they like and know.** If you cannot afford to pay to go to an event, offer to volunteer to help at check-in or help set up. Organizations understand that there are unemployed people coming to these meetings to network.

Business networking groups: These groups could be the local Chamber of Commerce. They could be a group of businesses that get together to promote leads to each other and help each other. Most of these people are working—get to know them!

Other networking groups: Your college alumni association or fraternity or sorority may have a chapter in your area. If not, organize one. There may be a young professional group or a group of ex-company employees or a group of retirees from a company. There are lots of groups: a good place to find many groups is a website called www.Meetup.com or on CareerDFW.org under the group tab.

Accountability groups: You need to have a person or a few people (never more than three or four) who will hold you accountable to keep you moving toward your goal of finding a new job.

Your spouse should NOT be in your accountability group. You want an unrelated person(s) to be your accountability partner(s). Your partner(s) may or may not be unemployed.

You should get together once a week (usually at the beginning or end of the week), either in person or on the phone to go over what you did last week toward your job search and what you plan to do this week. You are reviewing goals for the previous week then setting goals for the current week.

What are your goals?

How many calls will you make? How many informational interviews will you have? How many jobs will you apply for online this week? How many networking groups will you attend this week? How many professional groups or Chamber of Commerce meetings will you attend?

You make up the goals and then your partner will hold you accountable for them the next time you get together.

Always carry a name tag with you.

Are you in sales and marketing?

Trick question. YES you are if you are looking for a job. You are selling YOU and marketing YOU. Take a name tag with you when you go to networking events, professional group events, job fairs, etc. Keep one in your car and one in your briefcase.

In the past couple of years, I have attended over 20 job fairs and seen more than 6,000 people at those events. Of the 6,000 people looking for a job, I do not believe that I saw more than 30 people with name tags. I can remember the woman who had the dress that was too tight, the guy with the orange tie, and the woman in 8-inch heels. I do not know their names, but I know what they looked like. If they had a name tag, I could have put a name to the face or outfit.

I have talked to many recruiters who attend these events. They tell me that a name tag makes a huge difference. You have made it easy for the recruiter to put a name to a face (that person will see hundreds of people in a day). You want to make it easy for someone to remember YOUR name and face.

What should be on your name tag? Your first name in large print (72 pt.), your last name in smaller print (48 pt.) and what you do (your profession) below that (in 14 to18 pt) belong on your name tag. When I say large print, I mean large enough to be seen 10 or more feet away.

Where do I wear my nametag? You want to wear it on the upper right of your body as close to your neck as possible. Why? When you shake a person's hand, you shake with the right hand, so if your name tag is on your right, their eyes move up the arm they are shaking to the nametag and then to your face.

There is no need to buy a name tag holder (you cannot buy just one: you have to buy a package of them). Look through your drawers or desk. Have you gone to a convention? They gave out badges—use one of those. If you have to buy some, I recommend the 3 inch by 4 inch clip style name tag holders. And when you have your name tag, you can put some business cards in the holder. You never know when you will need one.

Do not buy or use name tag holders on a chain or cord. This puts your name tag in your belly area. If you are a woman, do not put a man in the uncomfortable position of having to look down at your name tag. Put it up next to your face. Also, name tags on a chain or cord, tend to flip around in the wind. Half the time, your name is against your body and cannot be seen by others. If you have to use a name tag on a cord, be sure to put your name on both sides, so if it does flip everyone can still see your name.

I use a three inch by four inch clip style nametag holder and I have a couple of versions of name tags in it. One for CareerDFW.org, one for CareerUSA.org, one with just my name and profession (that I use at networking meetings) and one with my name and college degrees that I use when I represent my school at local college fairs. And I always have a few business cards in the holder also.

Always carry business cards with you.

We just talked about putting a few cards in your name tag, so you are always prepared to sell yourself. If you do not have your name tag with you, you should always carry business cards with your information everywhere you go.

Restaurants, groceries, the gym, when you're on vacation—no matter where you go, you never know where you may strike up a conversation and need to hand out a business card.

What do you put on a business card? Your name, contact info, phone number, email address, LinkedIn information, and your profession or what you want to do. There is no need to put your home address. There is no need to put the words "email" or "phone". Use your cell phone number as your primary phone number and put only this number on your card.

At the beginning of a job search, I recommend that you do not get professional cards printed. I recommend using Avery #5871, white, two-sided, clean perforated cards. They come in sheets of 10 that you can print on your printer. You can download hundreds of free templates from Avery's website on the internet. All you have to do is add your information and print.

Have you received a business card from someone else and really liked the layout, text or graphic on the card? I only print a few sheets at a time. This way if I want to change something on my card, I do not have to throw away 150 cards. In addition, I carry a couple of different cards with different information on each.

Here's another hint about business cards. Keep **your** cards in one pocket and put the ones you collect **from others** in a different pocket. Have you ever asked someone for a card and they pull out a clump of cards and flip though them to find theirs? It does not look professional.

Also, get a vinyl or leather carrying case so your cards look great without any creases.

Have your 30 second intro ready.

When you meet someone and they ask, "What do you do?" what do you say? You have to be prepared to give a short and concise answer. If they want to find out more, they will ask you.

The idea of keeping the presentation to 30 seconds is to get their attention, make them curious and respect their time. You will need to adjust your 30-second introduction depending on the situation (e.g. social event, networking meeting, interview). Your social circle may not understand a technical term. When you are at a professional group, however, you can use those technical terms for that profession.

I want to concentrate on the networking format since that is the one you will be using the most.

I suggest the following format:
- I am…
- I do…
- I help…
- I need contacts at…
- I am…

Let's take a look at each part:

- **I am…**

State your name

"My name is _____ *"*
Say your first name, pause, then say your last name.
That way your name is distinct and clear.

- **I do...**

What do you do? What do you WANT to do?

You want people to understand what you do so they can help you if the opportunity arises. PLEASE keep your details looking <u>forward</u>. Phrases like *"my background is ..."* or *"for the past 20 years I have ..."* or a list of all the companies for whom you have worked does not tell someone what you can do for a new company.

- **I help...**

What skills or passions do you have that can help an employer?

What do you love to do? (At work, not personal things) Examples: *"I provide solutions for ...," "I lead sales forces ...," "I develop ...," "I am an individual contributor ...," "I am a team leader ...," "My passion is to ..."*

- **I need contacts at...**

What are your target companies?

Tell us what you need help with. If you filled out an application or saw a job posting online, that is your target company. Being specific will get you more help and more contacts. (You never know who <u>they</u> know unless you ask!)

- **I am...**

Say your first name, pause, then say your last name.

State your name again in case they did not hear it the first time. Many people may not catch your name at the beginning and may not ask to hear it again, so by repeating it at the end, you help the person you are talking to.

Many people start by saying, "My name is and I'm a (insert job title here)." Giving a job title, however, might limit you in the employer's eyes if they don't have a job with that title. You might say, "I'm a seller or outside salesperson" rather than "account executive" or "marketing consultant."

Some people prefer to say how they help companies at the beginning and maybe give a job title at the end when they repeat their name.

Pretend you are talking to your next boss (you may be!). Or pretend you are talking to the person who will forward your information to your next boss. The most important item is your name.

The second most important item is your profession, tied with the help you need on a target company.

There is no right or wrong way to do this. You have to be comfortable with what you say and how you explain it to others. I always recommend that you make sure your 30-second introduction is SO easy to understand that the cashier at the grocery store understands what you are seeking. Cashiers meet a lot of people each day—one of them might be your next boss!

Sometimes a good catch-phrase or slogan will help someone remember you. Be sure to present your introduction with a smile and vigor because it gets people to want to help you. And the last thing you should say is *"Thank you."*

Once you have your introduction written down, it's time to practice, practice, practice. WHY??? Practice so you can feel comfortable enough to look them in the eye, be aware of your surroundings and be able to smile while talking. Practice and ask for feedback.

Your introduction is not set in stone. You will change it many times until you are really satisfied with how it sounds. You will hear other people give their introduction and you may change yours when you hear a good phrase or keyword that did not come to mind.

Do not forget to exchange business cards.

Be very clear about what you are looking for when you ask for help.

How many times have you heard, *"If you hear of anything, please let me know,"* **Anything** could be a lot of things.

You have to be focused when you ask others to help you. Tell them what you want to do. Be specific. Most people are not mind readers. We cannot guess how you feel or what you want unless you tell us.

You may ask me for a drink. But if you are not specific, you could wind up with a soft drink a beer, a diet drink, an orange drink, a cola drink, etc.

If you want people to be able to help you, you have to take the thinking out of it for them. Tell them exactly what you want or exactly how you'd like them to help. Those who are inclined to do so, will. The others you won't convert regardless.

Be focused and specific (as specific as you can be). I know there are many 50 and 60-year-olds who do not know what they want to do when they grow up, but that is for another book.

Between 8 a.m. and 5 p.m. only go to a maximum of two to three networking groups per week, where most of the people are unemployed.

In the Dallas/Fort Worth area we have more than 75 career networking groups for the unemployed. Sometimes I think there are too many because I will see some people go from group to group. I wonder when they have time to look for a job. At the beginning of your job search, try many of them, but after a few weeks, pick out a few to go to each week.

You can and should go to as many professional or business groups as you can, because many of the people attending are working. They will be your best contacts.

Network with friends and family.

You are missing a large group of the people who know you best if you do not network with friends and family.

Twenty years ago, it may have been embarrassing to let your friends and family know you were out of work. But in today's society, everyone knows more than one person who is out of work.

In 2011 and 2012, it is reported that the actual unemployment number could have been as high as 16 percent. That is one person in every seven people you see.

You need to let your friends and family know how they can help you. Do they really know what you do? Explain it to them in plain terms. Keep it simple. If they want to ask more, you can give them more details.

Send out an email once a month giving everyone you know an update. It does not have to be long...maybe something like this:

> Friends,
> I want to give you an update on my job search.
> I would like to thank the following people for leads and suggestions this past month: Sue S., Mary H., Tom R. and Sam K.
> Just a reminder I am looking for a position in the _____ field as a _____.
> This month I am targeting the following companies: Acme Inc., XYZ Inc. and Health Inc. If you know anyone who works at one of these companies, or a similar company in the same industry, please let me know.
> Many thanks

The email needs to be brief and to the point.

Thank those who have helped you, remind people what type of position you are looking for and let them know your target companies.

You may want to send out two or three versions of this—one to family, one to friends and one to professional contacts.

BE SURE to send the email by putting the addresses in the BCC field so no one knows who else you sent the email to AND to protect others from their personal email address being sent out to those they do not know.

My wife did this during her last job search, every three weeks, and every time she sent out an update, within 60 minutes, she would receive a phone call or email with assistance. It works!

It also saves your family and friends the embarrassment of having to ask you how the job search is going if it is taking a long time.

Dress for success—shine those shoes, dress nicely and look good. Keep your style up to date (glasses, shoes, hair).

If you want to be amazed, go to a job fair, stand off to the side and just watch the people. It is astounding what someone will wear to a job fair or job interview. I have seen woman in 6- to 8-inch heals who can barely walk. I have seen dresses SO tight, that the women must have had assistance pulling it on. I have see men holding up the front of their pants and walking around with their pants drooping and their underwear showing.

For any job fair or interview, always be in your Sunday best! No matter what the company says, men should wear a coat and tie (suit) and women should wear a suit or nice dress (not revealing).

Men, gray, blue or black as the suit colors of choice. Make sure your belt and shoes match. Wear solid-colored socks and make sure they are long enough so when you sit and your pant leg raises, your skin does not show.

For women, the safest attire is a dark-colored skirted suit. Wear conservative, minimal make-up, minimal jewelry, little or no perfume. Shoes should be closed-toe, no platforms or high heels. If you are wearing pantyhose they should be clear or tan. Carry a briefcase or portfolio and leave the purse at home. You do not want to have all your hands full when you meet someone. Showing too much skin is never a good idea.

When did you last get new glasses? Are they up to date? Ask some of your most fashionable friends for their honest opinions.

Do you need a new hairstyle? Be sure your hairstyle is up to date by asking others. Do not go to an interview needing a haircut.

I once heard a speaker tell this story. He was asked to come in for an interview. The company told him they dress casually (golf shirt and khakis). He showed up in a suit and tie. The interviewer said, "You did not listen, we dress casually here." The person looking for work said, "I have not yet earned the right to dress like everyone here. I'm here to interview for a job."

I know of one interviewer who told me the first thing he does is look at a person's shoes. If they are not polished and shined, the interview is over quickly (and they do not get the job.) This person hires people for retail jobs.

Remember, an interviewer will form an opinion of you in the first three to five seconds after they meet you. There is no reason to let your appearance put you in a hole before you even have an opportunity to speak.

Job fairs—To go or not to go? ... that is the question.

I go to many job fairs each year to promote CareerDFW or CareerUSA. I talk to thousands of people each year. People ask me if they should go to a job fair.

Here is what I tell them: You want to find out what companies are going to be at the event. If you are targeting that company, then YES, you should go. If the company is going to the job fair, and you want to work for them, here is an opportunity to have a face-to-face meeting with someone from the company. It may not be the hiring manager, but you get to meet someone on the inside.

Two real job fair stories

First story: At a job fair there was a very long line at one booth. Forty to fifty people were waiting to talk to the representative from DFW Airport. Their workforce is in the thousands and they are one of the largest employers in the DFW area. The CareerDFW booth was close to the end of this long line. I asked someone to find out what they were giving away as they had the longest line, at least 10 times longer than any other booth. I told this to a couple of different people. When the first person got to the front of the line, he was told by the DFW Airport representative, "Check out the jobs online, and apply on line." That person had spent 30 to 45 minutes waiting to find out what we all know.

Another person who was also waiting in line got to the front and the representative told him, "Check out the jobs online, and apply on line." He said, "Thanks, but I have already applied for a job as a XXXXXXX. Do you know who the hiring manager is?" The DFW Airport representative, thought for a second and responded, "Yes, his name is Tom Smith and his number is xxx-xxx-xxxx." SCOOOOOOOOORE! This guy hit the jackpot. He now had a name and phone number.

So if the company you are targeting is going to be at job fair, go and try to make a contact.

Second story: When I go to job fairs to talk to job seekers about CareerDFW or CareerUSA, I always get volunteers from the community to assist me. At a job fair that was close to downtown Dallas, one of the volunteers decided to walk around to see which other companies were at the job fair. She told me that she checked online to see who was at the event and none of the companies caught her eye. All of a sudden, I see her walking quickly back to our booth where she got out her portfolio, took a copy of her resume and hurried back across the room to one of the booths. When she came back, she told me she had struck up a conversation with a recruiter at one of the booths and they said they were interested in talking to her. A few days later, she called me to tell me the rest of the story.

The job fair was on a Tuesday. She received a call the next day asking her to come in for an interview the following day. While she is driving home from the interview, the company calls her on her cell phone and offers her a job and they wanted her to start immediately.

But there is MORE to this story. She also told me if she had known the job fair was downtown, she would not have volunteered, because she lived over 20 miles away. But because she did volunteer and not back out, she found her next great opportunity and was working in less than 6 days.

Right place, right time.

An interview is **NOT** an interrogation but a two-way conversation.

An interview is not a one-sided event. The interviewer does not get to ask all the questions. You get to ask some also. You need to be prepared with at least 10 questions that explore areas YOU want to know about. The interviewer may cover some of these, but they will never cover them all. Most interviewers will ask if you have any questions. This is YOUR time to shine.

"What work issues keep you up at night?"

"When I am hired, six months from now when I am reviewed, what would you like to be able to say are my one or two greatest accomplishments?"

These two questions will tell you what has to be tackled first when you start the job.

A few other great questions:

How will my performance be measured? 30/60/90/120 days/1 year

Did we accomplish what you intended for today's meeting?

For salespeople: How do you feel about me for this position in comparison to others you have spoken to?

What kind of skills do you feel are necessary for a person to be successful in this job? Take notes and then proceed to demonstrate how you have every one of those skills.

Who do you know that I can talk to?

About what?? I know lots of people, but I can guarantee you that I won't refer you to any of them if you don't give me some indication that you have a direction in mind for the conversation. Because nothing is more valuable to me than my reputation, with my contacts being a close second. Any referral I give to you will reflect directly back onto me.

So before I connect you with any of my contacts, you need to convince me that you will leave a good impression because I will need to contact that person again one day.

All the time people say to me, "I'm looking around; do you know of anything?" I'll ask about what they're seeking and they'll say something like, "Well in the past I've done X, but I'm open to anything." There are no hiring managers seeking ANYTHING. They are seeking something, and if you can't articulate it for yourself, you are not ready to network.

You must first establish a direction and then go forth.

Can/Do/Fit

Have you noticed that you never get hired with just one interview? Usually it takes at least two and most likely three or more.

Can—The first phone or in-person interview is usually done by the HR department. They are trying to figure out if you "can" do the job.

Do—The second interview is usually with a hiring manager to see if you have the skills to "do" the job. This is where you need to decide if you want to do the job.

Fit—This area is usually covered in the third interview and is the one that trips up people up the most. Everyone has practiced interviewing, but the "fit" interview may be the one where you get to meet your hiring managers, boss(es) and maybe even several members of the team. They may never ask anything about your resume, but they may ask about what you do outside of work. Do you like the local sports team? Do you play recreational sports? They are trying to see if you will "fit" into this organization, whether you get along with others on the team.

Note: Are the above questions even legal? That is for another book. Depending on the interviewer, some have been trained by their HR departments on what to ask, while other interviewers have no training. You need to be prepared to answer whatever the question may be. If you do not feel comfortable with the questions they ask, you may not be comfortable at this company.

Can you do the job? Do you want to do the job and do you have the skills? Do you fit into this organization? I am sure you have worked at a job where there was someone who kept throwing monkey wrenches into the mix. Or where someone would not share important information that other people needed. The 90-day probation period (which is now being replaced by a 90 to 120-day contract in many places) is to make sure you Can/Do/Fit.

If you do not, they will look for someone else.

When you were a finalist and then rejected (you were #2 or #3), send a follow-up email 60 days later.

Did you make it to the finals for a new opportunity? Did you come in second or third? Do not give up and do not be mad. You still have a chance at the position.

First, be sure to send the hiring manager and HR people a thank-you note (in writing and sent U.S. mail) thanking them for the opportunity and wishing them and the company well.

Second, mark your calendar for 60 days from today to send a follow-up note. Why? We just talked about Can/Do/Fit. If the person they hired did not fit or they found out he or she could not do the job, you could be their white knight.

You did make it to the finals, but they selected someone else. Now, 60 days later, you send them an email stating that you are still interested in a position with the company. Maybe the company is not sure they hired the right person or perhaps another position opened up. They already know you. Your timing may just be right.

I have seen this work for job seekers.

Do NOT answer a call if you're in a loud, busy place. That is why you have voice mail.

You do not have to answer every call that comes in. If you are driving or in a loud place or in a crowded situation, it is OK to let the call go to your voice mail (if you have it). Just be sure you know how to access your voice mail.

I loved watching my mother-in-law when she got her first cell phone. It would ring and she would have to dig around in her purse when she realized it was her phone going off. By the time she got it, the call had gone to voice mail or they hung up. She would not wait to see if the caller had left a voice mail. She had to call the number right back (even if she did not realize who it was), just to find out who wanted to talk to her.

Voice mail is a good thing. If you do not recognize the number, better for the call to roll into voice mail than to answer it in a loud place or if you are driving. Let the person leave a message and number and then call back when you can be a professional seller. It also gives you time to do a little research if needed.

What are you selling? You're selling YOU!

Try to use a land line with a headset for a phone interview, not a cordless phone.

When you are going to do a phone interview, you want it to be successful. The last thing you want is for the line to go dead. A few years ago, I was on a phone interview and about 10 minutes into the interview, the power went out for just a second (it was a bright sunny day). The portable phone I was on went dead. Thankfully the interviewer called me back.

This has only happened to me once, but from my manufacturing background, I have learned that if you can eliminate a potential problem from happening in the future, you do it.

So, in order of best to worst options:

1) Use a hard-wired phone with a good quality headset.
2) Use a hard-wired phone without a headset.
3) Use a portable phone with a good quality headset.
4) Use a portable phone.
5) Use a cell phone with a good quality headset.
6) Use a cell phone.

The cell phone is at the bottom of the list? Yes. You know how easily a cell phone can drop a call or drop out if you raise your right hand 4 inches above your left shoulder on Mondays (you get the point).

Be sure to ask the caller if they can hear you clearly.

Do not let the phone call get in the way of your interview.

When doing a Web interview, have a clean desk, and clean background (and know what is behind you).

More and more interviews are being held using Skype, Google+ or other video chat software.

You need to practice video chatting with your family or friends BEFORE you have an interview with an employer. You need to think about what the person on the other end can see. What are they looking at behind you? Where do you look when you are video chatting? How do you sound?

I put some yellow tape on the camera or place a target with the camera in the middle. This reminds me where to look. I have a plain wall behind me for a background and I am aware that the other person cannot see my desk or where my resume, interview questions and a notepad are.

This is a true story. I know of a person who was doing a web interview. His desk was up against a wall so you could see the most of room behind him. The room was neat, but he was not prepared for his wife to walk into the background wearing no clothes. The person did not even know, but the interviewer said that he needed to start the interview over since they were recording the interview and could not have a naked lady in the recording.

Practice, practice, practice before you have to do it for your career.

Section Four

Interviewing

Conduct informational interviews.

You do this every time you talk to someone. You are getting information. The difference between an interview and an informational interview is that YOU are in control of an informational interview … you are asking the questions.

The following document is from Dennis O'Hagan. Dennis has taught informational interviewing for many years to career seekers in the DFW area. Dennis tells career seekers that they should read over the handout before the interview. He advises not stapling it so you can easily get to the next page. (Dennis throws the page on the floor when he is done with it and moves on to the next when doing a phone informational interview.) You can find the original five page handout on the CareerDFW.org or CareerUSA.org website. Just enter "informational interviewing" in the search box.

Many thanks to Dennis for allowing me to share the following handout.

NETWORKING: THE INFORMATIONAL INTERVIEW

What is an Informational Interview?

An informational interview is a meeting that you initiate for the purposes of gaining additional knowledge from a person with hands-on experience. In contrast to a job interview, you are the interviewer—the ball is in your court as to the content and flow. You need to come prepared with questions that you want answered. **Never, never ask for a job** when you have booked an appointment for an informational interview. There is no quicker way to alienate this contact and the person who gave you the referral than to have a "hidden agenda." Always follow up the interview with a thank-you note in which you reiterate anything you found particularly interesting or helpful. Also, keep a record of names, dates, comments and referrals.

Why do an information gathering interview?

- To get first-hand information from an expert;
- To check out if your assumptions about a career are really the truth;
- To get up-to-date information regarding trends
- To get more specific information on just about anything;
- To get more personal and subjective information;
- To get more reflective information about the on-the-job atmosphere, demands, joys, sorrows, etc.:
- To receive an assessment of your aspirations, your skills, your strategy, your resume, etc.;
- ...and anything else you can think of.

65

What is the difference between an informational interview and a job interview?

- **Control:** The balance is in your favor. You know what information you want and what the questions are.
- **Purpose:** They're not interviewing you for a job (not now at least), but you are making that critical first impression which could lead to other recommendations (one of your questions should be to ask for these), or perhaps a position with the company (only if they initiate the subject).
- **Pressure:** There is every reason for both of you to be relaxed. This is an opportunity to investigate just what you want. The spotlight is on your contact's expertise and your interest in that expertise.

How to arrange the interview:

- Personal referral is the most effective. Have a mutual acquaintance be the bridge for your contact.
- Walk-ins or phone calls are the next best routes if you don't have a personal referral.
- Letters seldom work unless they include a personal referral and follow-up by phone.

HOW TO ASK FOR AN INFORMATIONAL/REFERRAL NETWORKING MEETING

Four Approaches

- **The "Joe Smith suggested I call you" approach (with a referral)**

  "I was speaking with Joe Smith the other day and he suggested I contact you. I'm in the process of making some important career decisions and he felt you might be able to give me some valuable advice. My purpose in requesting a brief meeting with you isn't to ask for a position; I don't expect you to have or even know of an opening. My goal is to get some advice from you and some insight into the marketplace."

- **The "we have something in common" approach (without referral)**

  "I found your name and contact information on the _____ database. I'm in the process of making some important career changes and felt you might be able to give me some valuable advice. My purpose in requesting a brief meeting with you isn't to ask for a position; I don't expect you to have or even know of an opening. My goal is to get some advice from you, and some insight into the marketplace."

- **The "changing career direction" approach (without a referral)**

  "I am in the process of making some important career decisions and I believe your advice would be extremely helpful. I am trying to learn more about your industry or position to determine if it would be right for me. Your insight and experience could be very important as I make this decision. I would only need about 20 minutes of your time. Might we set up a meeting for next Tuesday or Wednesday?"

67

- **The "advice on my job search strategy" approach (without a referral)**

  "I am in the process of making a career change and hoped I might get an opportunity to meet with you for about 20 minutes or so. My purpose in requesting a brief meeting is not to ask you for a position; I don't expect you to have or even know of any openings. I would like to share my strategy with you and hear any suggestions you might have. Is there a time that is convenient for you to meet with me next week?"

HOW TO HANDLE INFORMATIONAL INTERVIEW OBJECTIONS AND BE PERSISTENT

Negotiate possible **roadblocks** in a polite manner and always use your judgment. Antagonizing someone who could have helped you is far worse than simply failing to meet him or her.

- *"I don't have time to see you."*
  - **I realize you are busy. That's why I am only asking for a few minutes.**
  - **Would it be more convenient for you to do this over the phone?**

- *"Just send me your resume."*
  - **I would be glad to; however, at this stage I am only looking for any information and advice you could give me that would help me direct my job search.**

- *"I do not think I can be of any help to you."*
  - **Joe Smith told me that you know a lot about_____.**
  - **I'm sure you know more then you give your self-credit for.**
  - **I'm sure you know more then I do about_____.**

- *"Sorry, we have no openings at present."*

- o I appreciate that: however, what I am currently looking for is information.

- *"I get a lot of calls from job seekers."*
  - o I'm sure it's because of your knowledge and experience. That's why I'm only asking for a few minutes of your time.

- *"Let me transfer you to the head of recruiting."*
  - o That would be very helpful, but would it be possible to spend a couple of minutes with you first to get some more specific advice and insight.

- *"I don't have any contacts to give you."*
  - o What I am looking for at the moment is advice and information. Your background and knowledge of the _____field is what I'm really interested in at this time.

Suggested Questions to Ask

- What keeps you awake at night?
- What are your greatest challenges today?
- Do you see your organization expanding its current service offering? If so, what are those new services?
- I've reviewed the information on the contract bid process. Who are your competitors and what are you doing better? Where do you need to improve?
- What are the trends? Are you expanding your market share?
- I've managed the results of customer surveys for process improvement and greater customer satisfaction. Do your members take an active role in market surveys, member councils and/or member task force activities?
- What percentage of vendors use your grievance process?
- Are you "delighting" your members? If not, where could you improve?
- What kind of training and background do you have?
- My expertise is in revenue enhancement, cost control and delivering exceptional service. I am a relationship manager. I achieve business objectives when working with sales, the customer and the internal organization to delight customers and meet corporate goals. Do you have any suggestions on my job search and how I might apply my skills to healthcare?
- Where can I gain additional information?
- Can you suggest anyone else that I should talk to? Can I use your name as a reference?

Some good questions with someone you know:

- What interested you in this career?
- If you were choosing a career today, would you make the same choice? Why or why not?
- What is most satisfying about your career? Do you enjoy coming to work everyday?
- If your son or daughter wanted to follow in your footsteps, what would you tell him or her?
- What are the most important qualifications to succeed in this job?
- What is your typical day like?
- What do you like most about this field? What do you like the least?
- What was your biggest success? Your biggest disappointment?
- What are the big issues in your field today?
- What are the major problems? Opportunities
- How has your field changed since you entered it?
- How secure is this field today? Is it growing or shrinking?
- How rapidly can someone expect to advance in this career?
- What can one expect to be doing and earning in two years? In five years?
- How much competition is there among your peers?
- If you could give me one solid piece of advice, what would it be?
- Is there anything else I should have asked but didn't?

"I really appreciate all this advice. It is very helpful and it should improve my job search considerably. Could I ask you one more favor? Do you know two or three other people who could help me with my job search? I want to conduct as much research as possible, and their advice might be helpful also."

"During the coming weeks, should you hear of any job opportunities for someone with my interests and qualifications, I would appreciate being kept in mind. And please feel free to pass my name on to others."

Read the letter from the president if the company is a publicly traded company.

When you are doing research on a company that is publicly traded, be sure to read the letter from the president/chairman in the annual report.

Why?

In most cases, it will tell you what happened last year and what the goals are for this year.

This is valuable information. If you know what the company's goals are, you can position yourself to help meet those goals when interviewing for an opening. These may not be the immediate needs of the hiring manager but will give you a great idea of where the company is heading.

Depending on how the interview goes, this could also be a great opportunity to ask something like, "I read in the annual report that the president is looking to (insert goal here). How is this division going to help attain those goals?" Or "What changes has this division had to make to help attain those goals?"

Number one, you have now shown that you did research into the company, and two, you may get a better understanding of what your goals will be when you get this position.

You can also listen to the quarterly analyst interview that most public companies hold. The CEO or CFO will share important information about the performance of the company. Many companies will have them on their website or you can listen live if you time it right.

Never say anything bad about a prior employer.

Keep it positive. When an interviewer asks you about your prior employer, you do not want to bad-mouth them.

If you bad-mouth a prior employer, who else will you bad-mouth? Employers want people who enjoy what they do, people who have a positive attitude.

Let's say you got laid off from The Magazine Company. You did not do anything wrong. More and more people were reading the magazine online, so they did not have to print as many. Because they did not have to print as many, you were laid off. Not your fault.

Do not tell the interviewer, "The company was mismanaged. They gave all the managers bonuses, but cut out the workers who really did all the work." Instead, say in the interview, "I really enjoyed working at The Magazine Company, but readership in the printed version was down, so the company had to right-size."

Turn whatever the reason was into a positive statement about your former company.

References—give them the heads-up when you give their names out.

"I had a great interview this week and gave my references to the company. Should I let my references know?"

The only answer is YES!

You may be asking, "Why do you say yes? I already got permission from the references to use their names." Yes, you did, but when you let your references know they may be contacted for a specific job, you are setting yourself up for success.

When you give your references to a company, send your references an email (or call them) as soon as possible (the same day) and let them know to whom you gave their name, the company and the position to which you are applying. Give your references a few talking points about the job or what you found out in the interview that your references could use in a conversation.

This is also a good time to make sure the references' contact info is still correct. Maybe someone is on vacation, in the hospital or on a project and will be inaccessible. Be sure to follow up with the person you gave the references to and let them know that person x is not available or person y has updated contact info.

Wouldn't it be great if the reference would say something like, "Joe is great. He really does a great job at x" (x being what keeps the interviewer up at night). Or "His best skills are x, y and z (x, y and z being a few of the key requirements of the job).

Your resume hooked the employer and got you the interview, and you did great in the interview. Do not drop the ball now. Make sure your references know what is going on. They may be able to help push you over the top to get the job by providing informed, pertinent information during the reference check.

Even if you have not given out your references' names in a while, you never can go wrong making contact with your references. Keep in touch.

Wouldn't you like to know why someone is calling you? Wouldn't you love to help someone who is using you for a reference by providing truthful information that is relevant? When they get a job, it is a great feeling to know that you helped someone.

"How is your relationship with your mother/brother/sister?"

Here is an interview question you may be asked. (Once again, I'm not sure if this is legal, but you have to be prepared.)

Why are they asking me this?

They want to know if you get along with people. Many people have a sibling or parent that they may not get along with, but there is no need to let the interviewer know this. They are now in your personal area. Even if you do not get along well, give them a positive answer: "We see each other for all the holidays." "We talk weekly."

The interviewer should not ask about your relationship with your spouse.

Do not get trapped by this question. Keep it positive!

Treat the receptionists and assistants well—they are the gatekeepers.

I have hired many people over the years. One of the most valuable positions in my company was the person who answered the phone and greeted the customers when they walked in. That person provides a company's first impression. They also are the first person you are going to meet when you arrive. They are the first person who will judge you on how you act and form an opinion quickly.

If you do not treat the person at the front desk with respect, believe me, they will let the hiring manager know. You want to be respectful and courteous to everyone. You do not need to chat it up with them. Just be appreciative of them.

At one company I worked for, when I would bring new people in for an interview I would usually walk them around (if I was interested in hiring them). I would introduce the prospective employee to some of the current employees. As soon as the interview was over, if the current employees did not seek me out to give me their opinion from a five to ten-second meet and greet, they would give me the thumbs up or thumbs down when I walked through the plant.

You are judged in the first five to ten seconds you meet someone. Make it count!

Keep your car clean. Someone may be sent out to check your car during an interview.
Clean car, clean desk = clear mind.

I have heard from several people who said the interviewer walked them out to their car to send them on their way. People thought this was a little weird.

Here is what is happening: The interviewer walked you out to your car to see if the car was neat and well kept. Why? If you have a clean car, the interviewer assumes you will keep a neat desk.

The interviewer may not be the one looking at your car. Maybe the secretary took note of what car you came in and someone else went and looked while you were in the interview. Even the guard at the security booth may be checking you out when you drive in.

If your car is a mess, it is a good sign that other parts of your life are a mess also.

Use a mirror when you do a phone interview.

When you are doing a phone interview, what do you look at? The telephone, your notes, your resume? If you have a mirror on your desk or the wall, you can check to see if you're smiling.

When you're smiling, you sound upbeat, friendly and professional.

Section Five

Other Tips

Insanity—Doing the same thing over and over and expecting the results to be different.

Do you do the same thing each week? Sit at the computer, looking for jobs online? Do you attend a career group each week, every other week or monthly? Does it seem like your job search is stalled? Are you getting any phone calls from companies or recruiters? Are you doing the same thing each week without any results?

If you are doing the same thing each week and you're still looking for a job six to twelve months later, something needs to change. Doing the same thing and getting the same results—nothing—indicates that you need to change what you are doing. It could be something small like changing some of the keywords on your resume or LinkedIn profile. Maybe you need to network with some new people.

If nothing changes, nothing changes!

Here is a list of things you could change in your routine:

1) Change your resume and LinkedIn profile.
2) Join different LinkedIn groups. (i.e. College, Alumni, Former Employers)
3) Go to different networking groups.
4) Find the professional groups in your field and go to those meetings.
5) Conduct informational interviews two or three times a week.
6) Volunteer for anything you have an interest in whether personal or professional.
7) Do whatever you need to feed your soul, i.e. attend religious services, develop a workout routine and stick to it, make lunch dates with friends.

8) Reward yourself in little ways that don't have to cost much, if anything. Go to a funny website and read some jokes, make a cup of hot tea, do your nails, get a haircut, spend a buck on Redbox and watch a movie tonight.

9) Start a blog. If you aren't ready to go public, then just start journaling privately.

10) Start a newsletter. If no one else has one, you can become the expert in the field.

11) Commit to reading books. Have a reading list and keep it updated. This is a great conversation starter because you can ask people, "What are you reading?"

12) Read articles about current ideas. LinkedIn is a great source for articles on business, various industries, tech trends, social media, and lifestyle information. This will help you stay current and be interesting to others.

13) Sign up for blogs that interest you. I find it helps me to limit myself to fewer than three at a time. Too much information is a distraction and will tempt you to spend too much time reading instead of putting into practice the ideas you are learning.

Keep improving your digital knowledge and skills. Don't just read about it. Practice it. We are all learning because it's constantly changing, so fight the urge to do it "perfectly." Just aim for practice, exposure and experience.

Do SOMETHING different!

Make sure you load your gun with all its bullets.

A Marine friend of mine tells this story "When you go into battle, you load your weapon with a full magazine." Would you carry a gun only half loaded? Of course not! The same goes for your job search.

You need to be doing everything you can to land that next great opportunity. You never know which bullet will hit the target, just like you never know which job search process will land you a job. You hope it is the first, but you need to keep you chamber loaded, just in case.

In the past few years, I have facilitated a career networking group. Hundreds of people have landed jobs and each story on how they did it is different. "Networking...a friend of a friend," "They found my resume on Monster," "They found me on LinkedIn," "I made a contact at a job fair."

There is no silver bullet, but you have to work every angle because you never know what might lead to success.

Volunteering is a great way to meet people. AND you never know who you will meet.

You are out of work so you have the time. Set aside a few hours a week to make this world a better place. There are thousands of ways you can volunteer. You never know who you will meet and what new skills you can share or learn.

I met a woman who had been out of work for eight months. During that period, she volunteered at a food bank. The food bank used a program called Salesforce to track the people who were getting assistance. She had never used the program before, but while volunteering she learned a new skill. She later applied for a job where they were using Salesforce, and because she knew how to use the computer program and they liked her, she landed her next great opportunity.

I know another person who was in construction management. He was looking for his next great opportunity and went to a local hospital where they were adding a new building. He volunteered in the building construction office for several months. The person in charge of the construction project left for another position and guess who got the open job? The person who had been volunteering for the past six months! He had the experience and knowledge and he showed it for free, and now he is getting paid to do what he does well.

Volunteer with a company that needs or uses your skill set. When a new opportunity comes up, ask for the interview. They already know your capabilities and you should be a top contender.

Exercise.

Yes, exercise is a very important part of your job search and your life.

First, it gets you out of the house. (If you have an in-house gym, get out of the house and go to a gym.)

Second, it is good for you. Most of us could afford to lose a few pounds.

Third, the gym is another place to network with other people. Go to the gym early in the morning or after work hours. Both of these times are when the employed work out.

Remember that the first impression you make with an interviewer is very important. If you are overweight or unenergetic, you may cost yourself a job before you even say anything. Working out will give you more energy that will show when you're talking to someone.

You have the time. Spend some of it doing something good for your body and health.

Read.

You cannot look for a job all day. Spend some of that time reading. Read items about your industry. Read books and blogs from the gurus in your field (and make comments.) It will help you stay on top of your game in your field. You want to stay up to date with the latest news. You may run across a great article that you can bring up in an interview. Or you can email that article to someone you had an interview with.

Another good reason to read is to fill your head with positive thoughts. Find a great book and read it. Don't just read articles. Reading a book is a greater commitment, does more for your attention span than simply reading blogs and articles and will give you more of a feeling of accomplishment, even if it's just for pleasure.

I know a person who was out of work for more than two years but was able to keep current with his technical skills. He read eight trade journals each month, and he knew what his industry was doing and was up to date with trends. The trade journals cost him nothing, this was a free way to stay up to date and be able to talk the talk. Find the trade journals in your field and get them online or in print. You may be able to find them at the library.

Reading also gives you content to update your LinkedIn profile. Add the Reading List application and include reviews.

Take a class or seminar.

You have the time. Do you have the job skills you need in today's world? Do you need a certification? Are you still using Microsoft Office 2003 at home? When you go to work, they most likely will be using the current version. You want to be able to jump right in at your new job.

You can take a class at a community college or university in your area. When you are on an interview and are asked, "What have you been doing since your last job?" you can tell them about the class or certification course you took and how it will help you and the company in the future.

CareerDFW.org and CareerUSA.org list several websites that have FREE online classes you can take. Just enter "FREE Classes" (with quotes) in the search box.

EVEN better—TEACH a class or seminar.

We all have something special we can share with others. More people will get to know you. This is a great way to keep your knowledge and skills up to date. You can become an expert as more and more people hear your information and come to know you as a thought leader in that area of expertise.

I know several people in the Dallas/Fort Worth area who have offered to give classes and seminars to other unemployed people to keep their skills fresh.

Teaching others or even speaking in front of groups is a tremendous confidence booster, which is very important during career transition. It will remind you of what do you know. It will help you organize your thoughts. It will help you to focus on what you excel at, which is always important to be able to articulate when asked, whether in interviews or just casually as you network.

We are in an action based culture now. You will be asked what contributions you make to an organization. You want to be able to say, "I wrote a lesson plan," or "I developed an organizational system and trained others to use it."

Hiring managers want people with ideas and people that are willing to take action. What better way to show you can do this than by keeping your skills current and sharing your expertise with others while you are in transition.

Spend time with your family and friends.

Once again, you have the time. This will give you the opportunity to get more involved with your kids' activities (you never know who you might meet … networking opportunities.) You can build great relationships during this time.

I once met a man who came to a networking meeting and told us what he was doing during his job search. He would get up at the same time that he used to get up when he was working, get dressed, eat breakfast, leave the house the same time everyday (just like he was still working) and not return until his normal time (just like he was still working). I did not know if he told his wife he did not have a job, but he said that he did not tell his kids and was keeping up the illusion that he was still working.

One, he was lying to his family. Two, he was not teaching his family a good lesson. I bet their lifestyle did not change and they were burning through money. Twenty years ago, you may have kept your job search a secret. Now the way to get a job is to let as many people as possible know about your job search.

Conclusion

As I said at the beginning of the book, I hope you can take something from these pages and apply them to your job search. There is no silver bullet or single thing you can do to get a new job. Everyone will find their next great opportunity in their own way.

Remember, if nothing changes (you keep doing the same thing each week), and nothing changes (you're not getting interviews), it is time to try something new.

Good luck with your job search!

Do you have a career tip that you would like to share?

Send them to YourJobSearch@CareerDFW.org along with your name, address, phone, profession and email address. I'll compile them and when we have enough I will put out another book called

MORE
THINGS I'VE LEARNED ABOUT
YOUR JOB SEARCH
THAT YOU MAY NOT KNOW

I will list your first name, last name initial, profession and your suggestion.

14563778R00055

Made in the USA
Charleston, SC
18 September 2012